LORD, HEAR OUR PRAYER

may the love of
God enfold you

Jenny Child

*To Canon David Adam
for his ministry over many years
and across thousands of miles
to my husband and myself
and for inspiring me to begin
writing modern prayers in
the Celtic Tradition*

Lord, Hear Our Prayer

by
Jenny Child
with a Foreword by
The Most Rev Rowan Williams,
Archbishop of Canterbury

the columba press

First published in 2011 by
the columba press
55A Spruce Avenue, Stillorgan Industrial Park,
Blackrock, Co Dublin

Designed by Bill Bolger
The cover photograph, taken by Ken Child, is of St Cuthert's
Island from Holy Island (Lindisfarne).
Origination by The Columba Press
Printed in Ireland by ColourBooks Ltd, Dublin

ISBN 978 1 85607 725 5

By the same author:
Celtic Prayers and Reflections
with a foreword by David Adam
The Columba Press, 2008
ISBN 978 1 85607 592 3

Contents

Foreword

by the Most Rev Rowan Williams, Archbishop of Canterbury

Jenny Child has already established herself as a writer of grace and charm, who is able to find words that will resonate with all sorts of people as they try to quiet their minds and open up to God.

Here are prayers for all kinds of situations – for the traditional seasons of the Christian Year, for moments of self-examination and struggle, for the ordinary joys and sorrows of each day, for children who have lost a pet and for deeper fellowship with the saints who have found and been found by God in the holy places of our islands.

Jenny offers us words of wisdom and deep feeling, and her book will be a great resource for all those who seek God in trust and humble love.

✠ *Rowan Cantuar*

Introduction

The words of the hymn 'prayer is the Christian's vital breath ... the soul's sincere desire' are as true today as when James Montgomery (1771-1854) wrote them so many years ago. Many people, including some Christians, live life at such a frenetic pace that time alone with God seems to be reduced to a bare minimum, if not squeezed out altogether.

We may forget God, but he doesn't abandon us. He is always ready to hear our prayers – in joy or in pain, in the good times and in desperate situations.

The early Celtic Christians saw God present, though unseen, in every activity of their daily lives. They affirmed God's all embracing love and protection even when experiencing the most dire circumstances, and entrusted their very lives to his care. They talked to God whatever they were doing.

The name 'Emmanuel' given to Jesus means 'God with us'. He is there with each one of us, with me. He has lived our earthly life with all its ups and downs, and knows the emotions we are experiencing.

It is my prayer that this book may encourage readers to form their own prayers and just to be still and know that God is with us.

Jenny Child

Morning Prayers

A New Day
Lord, you brush the sleep
From the eyes of the world.
As another day dawns,
You pull back the curtains
On a new day.
You open the shutters
On your Creation.
You give us the gift of a new day.
May we use it to your glory.

Hear Me, Lord
In the stillness of the morning
As the sunrise tints the sky,
As I see a new day dawning,
Hear me, Lord, O hear my cry.

May I use this day to please you
As I walk along Life's way,
That in all my thoughts and actions,
I might serve you day by day.

God's Gift –Today
As dawn breaks
and a new day begins,
I hear the birds
singing your praises,
and I see pink and gold clouds
scudding across the sky.
Only you, O Lord,
could create such beauty.
Help me to use this day
to your glory.

Every Day
I arise today
in your strength to uplift me,
in your power to direct me,
in your love to enfold me,
in your wisdom to guide me,
in your way to lead me
this day and every day.

Through the Day

In All Our Doings
In our comings and our goings,
Lord, direct us.
In our joys and in our sorrows,
Lord, share with us.
In our journeying and our homecoming,
Lord, protect us.
In our living and our dying,
Lord, be with us.

May God Find You
May the Seeking One, find you,
May the Welcoming One, receive you,
May the Redeeming One, save you,
May the Loving One, fill you,
May the Guiding One, lead you,
May the Living One, renew you,
May the Rejoicing One, delight you,
May the Grieving One, comfort you,
May the Protecting One, hold you,
And may the Father, Son and Holy Spirit
Bless you, each day, each night.

This Day and Every Day
May the strength of God, uphold us,
May the love of God, fill us,
May the wisdom of God, teach us,
May the light of God, guide us,
May the truth of God, enlighten us,
May the grace of God, save us,
May the protection of God, guard us,
May the freedom of God, liberate us,
May the presence of God, surround us,
This day and every day.

Day and Night
God of the day,
Guide me I pray,
God of the night,
Show me your light,
Kept by your might,
Each day, each night.

Always with Us
In our comings,
Be welcoming us,
In our goings,
Be guiding us,
In our grieving,
Be consoling us,
In our rejoicing,
Be celebrating with us,
In our journeying,
Be keeping us.

Be my Guiding Light
Lord, in the darkness
Be to me a light,
And in life's storms –
An anchor holding tight,
When there is sickness
Be my healing balm,
When I am feeling lost
Save me from alarm,
When the way ahead is dim
Be my guiding light,
When I am filled with fear,
Keep me day and night.

God of All Time
God of the sunset, God of the dawn,
God of the evening hour, God of each morn,
God of the day and God of the night,
God of each noon-tide, God of the light,
God of each hour, God of each year,
God of the future, yet God ever near.

In Every Circumstance
In our journeying
Be guiding us,
In our travelling
Be keeping us,
In our sleeping
Be resting us,
In our rising
Be refreshing us,
In our doing and our being
Be with us.

The Daily Chores
As I wash the clothes
Make me white as snow,
As I sweep the floor
Free my life from clutter,
As I send an email
May I pray for my friends,
As I boil water for coffee
Warm the coldness of my heart,
That awake I may watch with you
And asleep I may rest in your peace.

O Lord, Bless me
Bless me in my giving,
Bless me in my receiving,
Bless me in my rejoicing,
Bless me in my celebrating,
Bless me in my praising,
Bless me in my living,
Today, and every day.

Be with Us
In our living, guide us,
In our travelling, protect us,
In our working, inspire us,
In our resting, refresh us,
And in all our doings, be with us.

Lord, Guide Us
In our grieving,
Be cheering us,
In our ailing,
Be healing us,
In our praying,
Be hearing us,
In our living,
Be guiding us –
Each day, each night.

Night Prayers

Night Comes
Lord, you close the shutters on a weary world
As darkness falls.
You give us sleep to refresh us
And then you waken us to a new day –
With all its possibilities and challenges.
Whether we are awake or asleep we are yours,
Help us to live for you 24 hours a day.

As Night Falls
As twilight falls and night comes
and birds fly home to their nests,
May we be grateful for our homes.
May we find time for reflection
and relaxation within their walls.
May we rest in your peace
with our sins forgiven.
May your holy angels keep watch over us,
through the hours of darkness.

To Rest in Your Peace
I will lay down and rest in your peace,
With your angels guarding me,
With your love enfolding me,
And your presence surrounding me,
This night, every night.

God of Light
God of light,
You illuminate the night
with the radiance
of your presence.
Be with those who suffer pain
in the silent hours of darkness.
Comfort the dying and those
who watch with them.
Stay the hands of those
who are bent on evil deeds.
Give refreshing rest to those
who toss and turn in sleeplessness,
and give peace to your world.

For Slumber

Lord,

you bring down the curtain of night on a weary world.

Help us to commit our unfinished tasks into your hands

and lay our burdens at your feet.

Grant us refreshing sleep

that we may rise in the power of Christ,

to greet another day.

In Good and Bad Times

In Adversity
For those experiencing drought,
Hear us, good Lord,
For those who have lost everything
in floods or bushfires,
Hear us, good Lord,
For those whose loved ones
have been snatched away by disaster,
Hear us, good Lord,
For those suffering hunger and famine,
Hear us, good Lord,
For those whose countries are ravaged by war,
Hear us, good Lord,
In your mercy, encompass those in any kind of trouble,
For your name's sake.

Be with Us

When we face difficult problems,

Be with us, Lord,

When we have to make hard decisions,

Be with us, Lord,

When we don't know who to trust,

Be with us, Lord,

When we face changing circumstances,

Be with us, Lord,

When we don't know which way to take,

Be with us, Lord,

When we feel confused about the future,

Be with us, Lord.

Victory Won

Lord, how aimlessly we wander
Through the days and weeks and years.
Help us just to stop and ponder,
You are there in joy and tears.
May we use each day with wisdom
In our time upon this earth,
Ever working for your kingdom,
Seeking to bring peace on earth.
When our days of life are over,
May we hear you say 'Well done',
Pain and suffering will be over,
Death defeated, victory won.

Adrift

At times I feel I'm drifting
Out on the lonely sea,
Sometimes I think I'm drowning,
O Lord, where can you be ?
You surely know I'm lonely,
Weighed down by care and strife,
Come, living Lord, and save me
And fill me with new life.
Lord, lift my sagging spirit
With your unfailing love,
Come and walk beside me,
And turn my thoughts above.

Living the Christian Life

Your Love and Light
May your succour strengthen us,
May your power protect us,
May your compassion comfort us,
May your love lift us,
May your light lead us,
And may your Spirit fill us.

God be in Me
God be in my living,
God be in my dying,
God be in my talking,
God be in my walking,
God be in my sleeping,
God be in my weeping,
God be in my caring,
God be in my sharing,
God be in my living,
God be in my dying.

Share with Us
In our celebration, rejoice with us,
In our sadness, comfort us,
In our loneliness, befriend us,
In our frustration, encourage us,
In our busyness, calm us,
In our joy, share with us,
In our lives, be with us.

Lead Us and Guide Us
May the light of Christ
Lead us,
May the peace of Christ
Calm us,
May the love of Christ
Fill us,
May the mind of Christ
Guide us,
And may Father, Son and Holy Spirit
bless us in all our ways.

The Right Road
Lead me in the path of peace,
On the right road,
In the steps of the saints,
In the way of your witnesses,
And at journey's end, receive my soul.

On the Journey
Is there purpose in my journey?
As I plod along the road,
Am I just a lonely wanderer
Burdened by Life's heavy load?
Yes, there's purpose in my journey,
For you walk the way with me.
Strengthen my resolve to follow,
May my footsteps steady be.
Help me, Jesus, just to trust you,
In the ups and downs of Life,
Be with me in good and bad times,
In my joy and in my strife.
Holy Jesus, walk beside me
Till I reach my journey's end,
Then in Heaven, Lord, receive me –
As my Saviour and my Friend.

For God's Peace

For Your Peace
In the midst of busyness
Help me to make time for you.
In the midst of noise
May I hear your still, small voice
In the midst of confusion
May I know your peace
Which passes all understanding.

This Holy Place
Thank you for this place of worship,
Where your holy saints have trod.
In the quietness of your presence,
May we find the peace of God.

Thanks for those who through the ages,
Worshipped here and knelt in prayer.
In the quietness of your presence,
May we know that you are here.

Muddled Mind

I feel I'm trying to deal with ten different things at once.
Unclutter my brain, O Lord, of the trivialities of life.
Help me not to get so stirred up over little details.
May I get my priorities right – to care about the things
that really matter and not to be side-tracked by
unimportant issues. Bring order to my life and breathe
peace into my soul.

'Peace, Be Still'

Lord, you calmed the mighty waters
and the raging of the sea.
Come now, O loving Saviour
and calm the storm in me.
Bring quietness to my soul, Lord,
And whisper 'Peace, be still'.
Then may your balm flow through me
With peace my spirit fill.

Just to Know

Lord, in the 'hub-bub' of daily life,
Help me to draw aside for moments
of reflection and refreshment.
May I be still and know
that you are God –
just to be still –
just to know,
you are God, my God.

For Inner Peace

Lord, I come into your presence
With all my hopes and fears,
Yet I know that you have led me
As I look back through the years.
I come regretting actions past
And kind words left unsaid,
Forgive the sins that haunt me still
And give me peace instead.

For God's Protection

Armed for the Fight
Lord, fill us with your Spirit
And arm us with your Word
That we may be defended
As with a mighty sword.
The helmet of salvation
As covering for our head,
And with your reassurance
There is nothing more to dread.
Protect us with your breastplate
And arm us for the fight
So we are always ready
To stand for what is right.

Keep Us
From danger, be shielding us,
From hunger, be sparing us,
From anger, be saving us,
And all for your love's sake, we pray.

God's Hand
With your guiding hand,
Direct me,
With your powerful hand,
Protect me,
With your healing hand,
Touch me,
With your nail-pierced hand,
Redeem me,
With your loving hand,
Receive me.

God's Constancy
Lord, you have been with me,
You are with me,
You will be with me –
From now to eternity.

Save Us and Keep Us
From danger be shielding us,
From harm be protecting us,
From sickness be saving us,
This day, this night,
Each day, each night.

For Guidance

Like a Shepherd
Shepherd-King your love is tender,
Caring for your wayward sheep,
Make us willing to surrender
To that love so broad and deep.

Lead us gently when we wander,
Seek us when we go astray,
Help us, Lord, your love to ponder
As we journey day by day.

When we fall into rough places,
Lift us with your loving arm,
When we kick against the traces
Save us then from sin and harm.

As we stumble by the wayside,
Bear us on your shoulders strong,
Walk with us and be our guide,
Save us, Lord, from sin and wrong.

Kept by Your Might
Lord, be to me a light
And keep me in your sight,
Defend me with your might
And arm me for the fight,
Help me to do the right,
And guide me, day and night.

Christ our Sustainer
Christ the Light of the World, direct us,
Christ the Bread of Life, nourish us,
Christ the Good Shepherd, succour us,
Christ the Life, the Truth and the Way, lead us.

For God's Assurance

We Come
Lord, we come into your presence
With all our cares and woe,
Give to us your reassurance
As on Life's way we go.

God's Kingdom First
Lord, we worry about so many things –
What will we eat?
What will we drink?
What will we wear?
Yet you who care for the birds
and who clothe the wildflowers
in a vibrancy of colours, you know our needs.
May we seek your kingdom first
before any other concerns.

A Tiny Candle
Lord, this candle stands before me
With its flickering flame,
So like my faith which often wavers –
Yet this candle warms me
And gives me hope,
In you, the Light of the World.

The Pilgrim's Assurance
Lord God, I don't know where I'm going,
I cannot see the way ahead,
The future's door is closed to me –
It is enough for me,
To trust your leading,
To feel your presence,
And to know that you are there
With me wherever I go.

Do Not Be Afraid
Be still, the Lord is with you,
So do not be afraid,
Know that he walks beside you –
For his glory you were made.

Be still, the Lord is with you,
He calls you for his own,
Know that he travels with you,
And you are not alone.

Be still, the Lord is with you,
Just trust his guiding hand,
Know that he journeys with you,
Into the promised land.

Blanket Cover
God of love, you wrap the countryside
in a blanket of purest snow –
to cleanse,
to cover,
to beautify.
May we remember that you have promised
to make our sins, though scarlet, like whitest wool.

There is Sunshine
Although dawn breaks cheerless for me this day,
The sun is shining somewhere,
Give me the assurance that you are with me
in the shadows as well as
in the sunshine of life.

You Welcome Us
Lord Jesus, you bid us come to you
with our burdens,
with our tiredness,
with our worries,
for you are gentle and loving and you promise
to give us rest.

Thoughts on Psalm 27
You are my light and my salvation,
Why should I be afraid?
You are the stronghold of my life,
On you my hope is stayed.
I will not fear what people do
to me, your servant, Lord,
I will just simply trust you,
Believing in your Word.
Teach me your way, O Father,
And lead me where you will,
Help me simply to wait for you –
Your promise to fulfil.
That I may dwell within your house
for all eternity,
and live to praise your name, my God –
this is my only plea.

Life's Tapestry
From the tangle of our lives,
you can weave the perfect tapestry
of our joys and sorrows,
our successes and failures,
our achievements and unfulfilled dreams.

For Forgiveness

Words and Deeds
For the words spoken
that would have been
better left unsaid,
Father, forgive.
For the words left unspoken
that should have been said,
Father, forgive.
For the deeds done
that would have been
better left undone,
Father, forgive.
For the deeds not done
that should have been done,
Father, forgive.
Lord, guard our words and our actions
that they may be guided by you.

Lord, Give Me Hope
Lord, I ask forgiveness for the past,
Inspiration for the present,
And hope for the future.

Forgiveness
Betrayed by a friend for thirty pieces of silver,
And denied by one closest to you,
Yet you forgave them.
So often we disown you and act as though
we didn't know you,
we let you down by our words and actions,
Yet you forgive us.
When we are betrayed by friends
and not supported by those close to us,
when we are disappointed by those on whom we rely,
May we too forgive.

Forgive Us, We Pray
For our deep-seated prejudices,
Lord, forgive.
For our long-harboured grudges,
Lord, forgive.
For our unwillingness to yield to you,
Lord, forgive.
For our determination to have our own way,
Lord, forgive.
For our harsh judgement of others,
Lord, forgive.
For our unconfessed sins,
Lord, forgive.

Father, Forgive
For our impatience and disobedience,
Father, forgive.
For our waywardness and hard hearts,
Father, forgive.
For the sharp word or the bitter taunt,
Father, forgive.
For our pride and stubbornness,
Father, forgive.
For our apathy and indifference,
Father, forgive.
For our selfish motives and lack of generosity,
Father, forgive.
Our past – forgive, our future – direct,
And the present (your gift), may we use
to your glory.

If Only

'If only' I had said or done,
so often I regret the past,
forgive me now, for your dear Son,
bring comfort to my soul at last.

That good deed let me do today,
The kind word spoken to some soul,
To live for you, my God, I pray,
Lord, may this be my constant goal.

Let me go from here, O Lord,
To follow you, my whole life long.
O God, I give myself to you,
Let 'Resurrection' be my song.

Openness to God

To Worship You
May your holiness stir our conscience,
May your truth nourish our mind,
May your beauty purify us,
May your love open our hearts
and may we worship you with our whole being.
(Based on a prayer by William Temple)

To Glorify You
Fill our mouths with your message,
Set our feet on your path,
Fix our minds on your Word,
Guide our hands by your will,
Open our hearts to your love,
That our lives may glorify you.

Fill Us and Inspire Us
Lord, may your love fill our hearts,
May our lips sing your praise,
May our feet walk in your way,
And may your Spirit inspire us
to live for you alone.

For Wisdom, Patience and Love
Mellow my thoughts,
Calm my emotions,
Fill me with your wisdom,
   your patience,
   your love.

Renew Us
Holy Spirit, you created order out of chaos,
Come, renew us.
You overshadowed the blessed Virgin Mary,
Come, renew us.
You turned frightened disciples into fearless witnesses,
Come, renew us.
Fill us, use us and renew the whole Creation, we pray.

Open Our Eyes
Open our eyes, Lord,
to your Creation.
Open our ears
to your Word.
Open our lips
to your praise.
Open our minds
to your inspiration.
Open our hearts
to your love.
Open our lives
to your Spirit.

Reflections
A sunset – vibrant colours
of gold and pink interwoven,
a quiet time of day –
to sit and think, to remember,
to ponder and perhaps regret –
so many things –
and yet to hope –
for another day,
of possibilities and opportunities,
of challenges to be faced
and difficulties to be confronted –
not in my strength, but in God's.

Fire from Heaven
Spirit of God, fill us with fire as at Pentecost.
Widen our blinkered vision
to embrace new possibilities,
open our world-weary minds
to your energising power,
soften our cynical hard-heartedness
with your expansive love,
unfetter the preconceived ideas which bind us,
that we may live in your glorious freedom
and in the power of Pentecost.

Open Us to Your Presence
Open our eyes to your Creation,
Open our ears to your voice,
Open our minds to your revelation,
Open our hands to your guidance,
Open our hearts to your love,
Open our lives to your life.

Lord, give to me
Lord, give to me a willingness to follow you each day,
And give to me an openness to hear you as I pray.
Lord, give to me a loving heart to walk the narrow way,
And give to me assurance – you are my strength and stay.

No Beginning and No End
God of history, reveal your truth to us.
God of infinity, may we know that you
are without beginning and have no end.
God of integrity, may we be honest in our dealings.
God of eternity, give us a glimpse of your glory.

Open my Eyes
O Lord, open my eyes to what I am.
Open my eyes to what I can be.
Open my heart to receive your grace
to realise your potential for me.

Power to Change
Spirit of God,
fan the smouldering embers
of our faith,
into the fire of Pentecost –
able to change
frightened disciples
into fearless people
ready to die for what they believed.
So transform our lives,
that we may shine
as Christ's lights
in this dark world.

Begin in Me
Lord, we ask for –
Peace instead of war,
Food instead of hunger,
Love instead of hate,
Generosity instead of greed,
Simplicity instead of materialism,
Truth instead of lies,
A just sharing of the earth's resources
and a willing heart to allow
change to begin in me.

The Love of God

For the World, for me
I kneel at the manger
And see the Christ Child born –
for the world, for me.
I kneel at the Cross
And see the Son of God crucified –
for the world, for me.
I kneel at the empty tomb
And see the Lord, risen from the dead –
for the world, for me.

God's Love
Your love is stronger than the mighty ocean,
far greater than the deepest sea.
Your love is not confined by borders,
nor can its bounds restricted be.
Your love encompasses both earth and heaven,
without beginning and without an end,
and yet your love is very personal,
inviting each to be your friend.

The Love of God

Lord, you give us many gifts. May we seek above all
to have love that is patient and kind, not jealous or proud,
not keeping a tally of past wrongs, but love that protects
and trusts and hopes. Love that forgives and forgives
and keeps on forgiving. Love that is greater than knowledge or prophecy – a small measure of your perfect love.

Jesus, You Love Us

Lord Jesus,
you opened wide your arms on the Cross
to embrace all humanity.
Draw us with the cords of love
that we may know you more clearly,
love you more dearly
and follow you more nearly
day by day.

Boundless Love
Boundless God, how deep your love,
Its depth beyond all measure,
For faith and hope and love you give –
With love the greatest treasure.

For love forgives so many times,
And covers every kind of sin,
The breadth and height and depth not known,
Of your great love so deep within.

Your love surpasses human thought,
Beyond each tiny, finite mind,
The love that led you to the Cross,
Salvation there for us to find.

O God, now fill us with such love,
A little portion of your own,
That we may praise your name always
And seek to follow you alone.

Enfold and Encourage
Lord, help me to enfold people in your love
And not try to exclude them.
May I not impose restrictions on that love
Which is stronger, broader, deeper
than my own narrow-mindedness.
May I make allowances for the strengths
and weaknesses of individuals.
May I seek to strengthen their faith
and offer them the same encouragement
that you give to me.
Lord, help me to be an encourager,
not an excluder.

Christ, the Good Shepherd
Hear the loving shepherd calling,
as he seeks his wayward sheep.
Follow him for he will lead you
with his love so strong and deep.
He still journeys through rough places
searching for the sheep that's lost,
home he brings it on his shoulders,
bought at such tremendous cost.
When he brings that sheep back with him,
all the angels then rejoice,
for the lost one has responded
to the Shepherd's tender voice.

For Healing

For the Medical Profession
Lord, you healed the sick, and the very touch of the hem
of your garment brought wholeness to the sufferer.
We pray for all involved in the medical profession:
For surgeons and doctors,
God of wholeness and healing, hear us,
For nurses and aides,
God of wholeness and healing, hear us,
For hospital staff and healthcare personnel,
God of wholeness and healing, hear us,
For ambulance drivers and paramedics,
God of wholeness and healing, hear us,
For helicopter pilots and rescue workers,
God of wholeness and healing, hear us,
For medical missionaries and aid workers,
God of wholeness and healing, hear us.

Your Touch
On those who are in pain,
Come, Lord, with your healing touch,
On little children suffering,
Come, Lord, with your healing touch,
On those awaiting surgery,
Come, Lord, with your healing touch,
On those depressed or anxious,
Come, Lord, with your healing touch,
On those troubled in body or mind,
Come, Lord, with your healing touch.

Care for Others

Love for My Neighbour
O God, help me to offer forgiveness
to my enemy,
tolerance to those who oppose me,
love to those who befriend me,
and to myself – respect.

The Homeless
The foxes have holes and each bird has its nest,
yet you, Lord, our Saviour, had nowhere to rest.
We think of the homeless and those sleeping rough,
we pray for each soul who is finding Life tough.
Lord, help them to trust you as Master and Friend,
for you walk beside them through life to its end.
O God, give to us the compassion we need,
and save us from scepticism as well as all greed,
that moved by your Spirit, we might happily share,
and filled with your love might show that we care.

For All Christians
Lord, we pray for all Christians,
May they stand firm in their faith.
For those who have left home
and family for your sake,
May they stand firm in their faith.
For those who are persecuted
for their beliefs,
May they stand firm in their faith.
For those who have lost everything
because they are Christians,
May they stand firm in their faith.

You Alone Know
There are so many people, Lord,
for whom I want to pray,
but you alone, know all their cares,
just help them on their way.
And some of those are suffering
from sickness, strife or pain,
but you alone, know all their cares,
Lord, make them whole again.
And others are in grief, O God,
without the one they love,
but you alone, know all their cares,
Our Lord in heaven above.
Yet other ones are lonely,
they feel they have no friend,
But you alone, know all their cares,
be with them to the end.

Hands
Hand can hurt, hands can heal,
Hands can harm, hands can help,
Lord, use my hands to your glory.

Lord, We Pray
Lord, we pray for all the peoples
in war-torn, ravaged lands.
Those who suffer persecution
strengthen by your powerful hands.
Lord, we think of all the hungry,
dying now through lack of food,
Make us conscious of their suffering,
use us now to do some good.
Lord, we call to mind the lonely,
losing homes and loved ones too.
Stir us, O God, to action
to see what we can do.
Lord, we pray for all the nations
and for peace upon the earth,
In each one see your image –
and recognise their worth.

To be Christ to Others
May I see Christ in others,
and be Christ to others:
The beggar sitting by the Cathedral gate
whom I would rather ignore.
May I see Christ in others,
And be Christ to others:
The person collecting for charity
when I don't want to stop.
May I see Christ in others,
And be Christ to others:
The woman doing a survey
when I'm rushing in my lunch-break.
May I see Christ in others,
And be Christ to others:
The old person wanting to tell me
their story for the 'umpteenth' time.
May I see Christ in others,
And be Christ to others.
Lord, give me grace to see you in others,
And to show your love to others.

In Sorrow

Be with Them
Saviour, with your heart so tender,
Come to those who grieve this day,
Those who mourn the loss of loved ones,
Be with them, O Lord, we pray.
And for those who suffer illness,
Come with healing touch this day,
Those who sit and wait in anguish,
Be with them, O Lord, we pray.
Man of Sorrows, loving Saviour,
Come with peace to those this day,
All who grieve and fear and worry,
Be with them, O Lord, we pray.

Stand by Me
Jesus, stand beside me
In my darkest hour,
Comfort and sustain me
By your mighty power,
When I feel that all is lost,
Enfold me in your love.
Come and walk, beside me, Lord
And lead me home above.

In Memory of Diana
How fleetingly our lives are passing,
Like candles flickering in the wind,
Or like the fading flowers falling,
To everything there is an end.
And yet, he rose to life victorious,
Triumphant o'er his earthly grave,
Though we to dust and ashes turning,
New life, new hope to all he gave.

On the tenth anniversary of the death of Diana, Princess of Wales

Creation

Abundance without Limit
Bountiful God, you lavished your creation
with exquisite beauty and infinite diversity.
May we see your handiwork in the tiniest
insect as well as in endangered whales
living in the oceans. May we delight in all
that you have given us and may we be
faithful stewards of all
that you have entrusted to our care.

Creation Abused
Creator God, you fashioned this world
to be full of beauty,
but we have spoiled it by greed,
exploitation and apathy.
Forgive us and help us all to feel
Responsibility for its welfare.
May we conserve,
  protect,
  and cherish
  its diversity and fragility.

Generous God
God of abundance,
Help us to share,
Help us to care,
And seek to repair,
Our mismanagement
Of this world –
Our world,
Your world.

Water
Water for drinking,
May we cherish it,
Water for washing,
May we not waste it,
Water for cleansing,
May we value it,
Water for irrigation,
May we conserve it,
Water for recreation,
May we appreciate it.
May we never take this resource
for granted, O Lord of Living Water.

Symbol of Life
A raindrop –
Forerunner of rain –
Symbol of life –
To those dying of thirst,
To the drought-stricken farmer,
To the desert plants,
Waiting to burst forth
In vibrant colour.
Lord, thank you for rain –
That precious liquid,
Without which we cannot live.

Creation – A Trust
God our Creator, you made everything to be beautiful,
but our sin has blighted your handiwork.
Give us a sense of responsibility
to care for your creation. It is a trust from you.
May we use the earth's resources wisely and fairly.
Make us good stewards of your bounty.

Thanks be to God
For the world that you have made,
Thanks be to God,
For the beauty of creation,
Thanks be to God,
For the joy of human love,
Thanks be to God,
For the day and for the night,
Thanks be to God,
For the sunshine and the rain,
Thanks be to God,
For the gifts that you have given,
Thanks be to God.

Lord of All
Lord, of the elements,
We offer our praise,
Lord, of the wind and rain,
We offer our praise,
Lord, of the snow and ice,
We offer you praise,
Lord of the sunshine,
We give you thanks and praise.

Our Responsibility
Bountiful God, you have given us so much,
May we be faithful stewards.
In the care of our planet,
We acknowledge our responsibility.
For our part in causing climate change,
We acknowledge our responsibility.
For the depletion of fish stocks in the seas,
We acknowledge our responsibility.
For careless consumption of energy,
We acknowledge our responsibility.
For the extinction of many species,
We acknowledge our responsibility.
For the misuse of resources,
We acknowledge our responsibility.
For polluting and exploiting your Creation,
We acknowledge our responsibility,
and ask your forgiveness.

Beside a Fjord in Spring
Lord, your majesty is seen here,
In snowy mountain peak,
In clear blue sky and gentle breeze –
Mysterious fjord deep.
The perfume of the fruit trees
wafts down the mountainside,
And wildflowers in profusion
are growing far and wide.
Creator God, you made this world
and set it all in place,
Help us to love and cherish it,
Great God of time and space.

God of Every Place
God of the heavens, you fling the stars across the night sky
like diamonds scattered on velvet.
You cause the moon to rise and the sun to set.

God of the earth, you lavish your creation with abundance
and diversity like the colours of the rainbow.
You make the day to dawn and the night to fall.

God of the oceans, you show your power
in the might of the waves,
in the lightning and thunder,
and yet, you are heard in the still small voice.

Eucharist

Strengthen Us
Lord of heaven and earth,
you give us bread
from the wheat of the field,
and wine from the grapes
of the vineyard.
As we eat this bread
and drink from the chalice of blessing,
may we be strengthened for our journey,
with this spiritual food.

Divine Food
You multiplied the loaves and fishes,
and changed the water into wine,
Come, Lord, as sacrament is given,
and feed us with the food divine.

This Holy Food
In this place of contemplation
where the holy saints have prayed,
may we bow in adoration
all our hope on you is stayed.
In the silence of the sanctuary
as bread and wine are given,
help us to find your peace, O Lord –
that special balm from heaven.
Then as we leave this sacred place
to journey on our way,
sustain us with this food divine,
as we live from day to day.

The Eucharist
You call us, Lord, to come apart,
just to be still and find you here,
to hear you speak in written Word,
to meet you here in broken bread
and wine outpoured to give us life.
We come with shattered hopes and dreams
and hunger for your healing touch.
Draw near to us, O Risen Lord,
'tis you who loves the world so much.

This Sacrament Divine
You call us, Lord, to come and share
this sacrament of bread and wine.
We come with Christians everywhere
to share this sacrament divine.
With cares and woes we come, O Lord,
and lay our burdens at your feet,
we praise your name and hear your word,
in bread and wine, yourself we meet.

Take and Eat
Draw near and take the broken bread
And drink the wine outpoured for you,
And look upon his thorn-crowned head,
For his remembrance, this you do.
Then feed upon him in your heart,
And as you walk along life's way
Be well assured that for his part,
He will be with you day by day.

Advent

The Second Coming
Lord, you are the desire of nations and the dayspring bright, and yet you came into the world as a tiny Baby born of a virgin. When you come again with great glory, may we be found awake and alert, ready to welcome you as King of kings and Lord of lords.

The Second Coming
When you return in glory, O Lord,
May we be ready,
Keep us watchful and prepared,
Ready to greet the Bridegroom
at whatever hour you may come.

Come, Lord Jesus
Come to the faithful, O Lord,
Maranatha, come Lord Jesus,
To the hungry and the dispossessed,
Maranatha, come Lord Jesus,
To the persecuted and downtrodden,
Maranatha, come Lord Jesus,
To the homeless and the refugee,
Maranatha, come Lord Jesus,
To the sick in mind, body or spirit,
Maranatha, come Lord Jesus,
To those who have lost everything in disasters,
Maranatha, come Lord Jesus,
To those who mourn the loss of loved ones,
Maranatha, come Lord Jesus,
To those who are dying,
Maranatha, come Lord Jesus,
When you come at the end of the world
in great glory on the last day,
May we be found watching and waiting
for your return,
Maranatha, come Lord Jesus.

Christmas

Deity in Human Form
Holy Child of Virgin born,
Wrapped in swaddling clothes so warm,
Come to earth to save us all,
Sleeping in a cattle stall.
God Incarnate now is born
Deity in human form,
He the Word made flesh for us,
Came to die upon the Cross.
Jesus will return again,
To begin his promised reign,
He the King – the Lord of all,
Once the Babe in cattle stall.

Christ in the Manger
See him in the manger lying,
Tiny Babe of Bethlehem,
Lord of life and death defying,
Christ the Lord, we worship him.

Shepherds come, a lamb they're bringing
To the Child in manger laid,
He of whom the angels singing,
Lamb of God – our ransom paid.

See the wise men in their giving
Of their incense, gold and myrrh,
Make us generous in our living,
Saviour Christ, Incarnate Word.

See the blessed Mary watching,
Caring for the Child she bore,
Now all peoples are rejoicing,
Christ the Lord, we him adore.

Such Wonder

Lord Jesus, you were willing to accept
The vulnerability of a child,
And to be born as a defenceless infant.
My mind cannot comprehend such a wonder –
That you the King of Heaven were prepared
To take our human form and come to earth,
Not as a conquering hero but as the Babe of Bethlehem.

At Christmas

May the spirit of Christmas fill our hearts
With great joy like the shepherds,
That we too may seek the Babe
Lying in the manger.
May the spirit of Christmas fill us
With generosity like the Wise Men,
That we too may offer our best
To the Holy Child.
May the spirit of Christmas fill our lives
With the obedience of Mary,
The joy of the shepherds,
The generosity of the Magi
And the peace of the Risen Lord.

All the Year
Lord Jesus, you went about doing good.
Especially at this Christmastide may we
Care for the lonely, share with the homeless,
Spend time with the aged,
Rejoice with the children,
Show love to all creatures.
Let this be our aim not just at Christmas
But every day of the year.

New Year

Tempus Fugit
How quickly time is passing,
The days and months and years,
As we look back remembering,
The joys as well as tears.
And now the New Year's coming,
What will it hold in store ?
The opportunity to serve you
And love you even more.

For the New Year
God of eternity, a new year stretches before us.
What will the future hold for us ?
Whether it brings sorrow or joy, sickness or health,
failure or success, may we know
that you hold us in the palm of your hand.
Help us to trust you in every changing circumstance
of our lives.

New Beginnings
God of new beginnings, you make all things new,
Yet you remain the same – yesterday, today and forever.
As we stand at the gateway leading to another year,
Give us the spirit of adventure to dare new things for you.
May we place our hands into your hands, knowing that
you will light our way into the unknown future.

One Day – A Thousand Years
Lord of all time, a thousand years are as a day to you.
We stand on the threshold of a new year
and come with regrets and unfulfilled dreams
and missed opportunities.
Give us grace to step out boldly in your strength
that we may live our lives to your glory
and in the sure knowledge
that you walk every step of the way with us.

Lent

Ash Wednesday
This cross of ash upon my brow,
A sign of grief for all my sin,
Before the King of Heaven I bow,
Forgive me, Lord, come live within
My heart so hard and cold,
Come, with your burning flame of love,
Forgive my wandering from your fold
And lead me on to heaven above.

Draw Us to Yourself
God our Father, you loved the world so much
that you sent your Son to die for us.
During this season of Lent,
may we draw closer to yourself
as we follow the way of Christ's death and passion.

This Lenten Season
Lord, in this season of Lent
may I be more aware
of my short-comings.
For the hasty word spoken in anger,
Lord, have mercy,
For the kind deed not done,
Lord, have mercy,
For thoughts that dishonour you,
Lord, have mercy,
For stubbornness and hardness of heart,
Lord, have mercy.
Give me the insight to see
what I am,
and the grace to become
what you would have me be.

Good Friday

Some Thoughts
Lord, you bore the sins of the world
And took its suffering upon yourself,
You opened wide your arms on the Cross
For us, for the world, for me.
Forgive our continued sin –
Both deliberate and unconscious.
Lead us back to your self,
Confront us with the Cross
And all that you sacrificed for each one of us.
Draw us to yourself –
To resurrection glory
And to newness of life.

You Died for Me
Lord Jesus, you died for the world, for me,
May I respond to that love.
You were betrayed and forsaken,
May I respond to that love.
You suffered the agony of Crucifixion,
May I respond to that love.
You bore the sins of the world on the Cross,
May I respond to that love –
So amazing, so complete that only
total surrender to your will is acceptable.

Easter

He is Risen
Born in a manger,
Mary's Child,
Himself a stranger –
Gentle, mild.
Nailed to a Cross of wood,
Mary's Child,
Christ, doer of good –
Pure, undefiled.
Rising to life that morn,
Mary's Child,
Lord of the Easter dawn,
Man to God is reconciled –
Alleluia.

The First Easter
Early in the morning on that first Easter Day,
Jesus rose triumphantly – victor o'er the fray,
Lord of life, the battle done,
Resurrection crown now won.
Early that same morning Mary came to mourn,
Little did she guess what joy
Awaited her that dawn,
So when she saw the 'Gardener',
She asked him had he seen
Her Lord and Master crucified,
Now missing from the scene.
So gently then, he spoke to her
And called her by her name,
And in that moment Mary knew –
Her life forever changed.

Alleluia to our King
Notes of gladness, hymns of praise,
To the Lord of heaven we raise,
With the angels let us sing,
'Alleluia' to our King.
Christ who conquered death and sin,
Let the King of glory in,
Fling the gates now open wide,
Welcome him to come inside.
He the first fruits from the dead
Christ, our God, the living bread,
Let us with the angels sing,
'Alleluia' to our King.

Baptism

A Baptism Prayer
As Jesus blessed the children,
Who came to him each day,
May he enfold you in his love,
In his own tender way.
And may our Lord, be always near
To guide you and to bless,
And may he fill your whole life long,
With peace and happiness.

As You are Baptised
Loving God, as we bring this child to be baptised.
We pray that you will bless, guide and strengthen him/her.
May his/her tiny footsteps follow your way
and may he/she know
that you are always there all through his/her life.

Baptism

God of love and God of mercy,
Bless this tiny babe we hold,
Guide, protect, uplift and strengthen,
Ever keep within your fold.
God our Father and Creator,
You who cause new life to be,
May this child now to you given,
Seek to serve you faithfully.
May the act of water sprinkled
Wash away all trace of sin,
As the Cross's sign is given,
May this child's new life begin.

Confirmation

Defend Your Servants, O Lord
As young people affirm the promises
made on their behalf at their baptism,
Defend your servants, O Lord,
As they face many temptations,
Defend your servants, O Lord,
As they seek to live for you,
Defend your servants, O Lord,
As they ask for guidance for their future,
Defend your servants, O Lord,
As they pray for the power
of your Holy Spirit to fill them,
Defend your servants, O Lord,
As they come to be confirmed,
May they know the depth of your love,
The assurance of sins forgiven,
The nearness of your presence
and the promise that you will be with them always.

A Prayer for those being Confirmed
Lord, we pray for those being confirmed,
May they stand firm in their faith,
When temptations come,
May they stand firm in their faith,
When they experience 'peer pressure' to do wrong,
May they stand firm in their faith,
When they are rejected by family or friends
for their Christian belief,
May they stand firm in their faith,
Confirm, strengthen and keep them
by your unfailing love.

Marriage

Jesus Joins You
As Jesus graced the wedding feast in Cana long ago,
So today he stands beside you to guide the way you go.
When life's 'a bed of roses',
He will share this joy with you,
And when your hearts are heavy,
His love will see you through.
For Jesus said of man and wife,
'The two shall be as one',
Commit yourselves to him this day,
And know that this is done.

As You are Married
Lord, we pray for these your servants
On their joyful wedding day,
Be with them in good and bad times,
Lead them on the pilgrim way,
May they have a steadfast patience
As they seek to live each day,
Make them loving and forgiving,
Lead them on the pilgrim way,
As they share their joys and sorrows
When these come from day to day,
May they know your loving presence,
Lead them on the pilgrim way.

The Church

The Body of Christ
God of the universe,
you called your Church to serve humanity
and to proclaim the Gospel.
So often it is persecuted and condemned
and sometimes, we have to admit,
apathetic and complacent.
Fan the smouldering embers of our faith
into the fire of Pentecost
that we may be your faithful witnesses in the world.

The Church's Mission
Lord Jesus, you gave your Church the commission
to preach the Good News of your Kingdom.
To baptise, teach and nurture all believers,
to respond to human need by giving loving service.
To seek to change unjust practices in society
and to strive to safeguard creation
and to hold it in trust for you.
Give us all grace
to be faithful members in our calling.

For the Church

Great Shepherd of your sheep,
we pray for your Church throughout the world.
You called it to be a witness to your truth.
Forgive our apathy and renew in us a sense of mission.
May both clergy and lay people
shine as your lights in a dark world,
for we are the Body of Christ.

For World Peace

That Change may Come
Holy Spirit, Comforting One,
Blow over this earth:
Where countries are greedy and affluent,
May they learn to share;
Where countries are ravaged by war,
May peace come;
Where countries are stricken by famine,
May their needs be fulfilled;
Where countries are proud and arrogant,
May they seek humility.
May your kingdom come
and may the earth may be filled
with the glory of God
as the waters cover the sea.

The Seasons

Through the Year
Sparse and bare all the Winter
Waiting for new life to come,
Green shoots now in Spring are showing,
Early signs of life begun.
Summer next explodes in colour,
In a blaze of every hue,
This then surely is the season
When there is so much to do.
Once again comes Autumn turning
All the leaves to burnished gold,
Then we stop and pause in wonder
At the glory we behold.
For the seasons that you give us,
Lord, we offer you our praise,
May we hold in trust Creation,
Faithful stewards, all our days.

Spring
Light is breaking,
Spring is waking,
From the gloom of Winter's night,
Bulbs are sprouting,
Children shouting,
Welcoming the days of light,
Birds are singing,
Signs are springing,
Everywhere –
To show new life.
God of all being,
Help us in our seeing,
To praise you, Creator,
The Lord of all might.

Holy Places

To Lindisfarne
This other worldly place,
Where earth is touched by heaven,
And light illuminates
with special brightness,
where twice a day
the tide comes in,
severing the island from the mainland,
and all is still and veiled
awaiting revelation.

This Holy Place
Lord, thank you for the privilege
of worship in this place,
for quiet contemplation
within this sacred space,
where saints throughout the ages
have knelt and lived and prayed,
with you our strong Defender
we will not be afraid.
Help us to follow closely
the path your saints have trod,
For every step will bring us –
nearer to you, our God.

This Special Place
A holy place where saints have lived
To serve God in their fellow beings,
Where prayers have risen,
Like angels' wings to heaven –
The gap from earth is tissue-thin
When music floats through ancient stone
To join with heavenly choirs.
A busy place of crowds and noise,
Where people come from many lands
To see this place where saints have walked
Encompassed by these sacred walls,
May they find God.
A quiet place to stop and pray
For peace and for our needs,
Whispered words of anguish
Or of thankfulness,
Through centuries long past
And still today,
The pilgrim, tourist visiting,
Pause in wonder and perhaps find God.

For All the Saints

Walk with the Saints
To follow the saints, Lord, let this be our aim,
To walk in their footsteps and honour your name,
That seeking to serve those we meet day by day,
May show Christ the Saviour, the Life and the Way.
Give us their tenacity to hold fast the faith,
In quietness and confidence, Lord, may we wait,
To see the revealing of your master plan,
And in its fulfilment, your own guiding hand.
Grant us their endurance to run in life's race,
To learn from example that aided by grace,
And standing secure and firm to the end,
In heaven we'll meet you, our Saviour and Friend.
Give us then the courage to follow their lead
With your grace supplying the strength that we need.
May we, Lord, be willing to die for your word,
'Well done, faithful servant',
This message is heard.

Those Irish Hills
Irish hills of softest green
where saints have knelt and prayed,
and misty rain still quietly falls,
as in those ancient days.
Still the people come to pray,
to feel the gentle breeze,
in these hills of emerald green,
dappled with the Autumn leaves.
To Ireland dear, St Patrick came
to preach and teach the word of life,
and yet those hills have also heard
the cries of agony and strife.
Lord, may we journey now in peace,
where saints of old have trod,
together then in harmony –
to live for you, our God.

The Saints of our Isles
Lord, for the saints of our Celtic isles,
We bring our thanks today,
For Patrick of Ireland preaching your word,
To lead folk to walk in your way.

To Iona, Columba came to live,
To teach all the people there,
And Aidan to Lindisfarne, Holy Isle,
Came to show them Christ's loving care.

And George of England, armed for the fight,
With the dragons of sin and wrong,
For all these your saints, O Lord, we would raise
Our voices in prayer and in song.

And David of Wales came to shepherd your flock,
He came with the good news to share,
Encouraging all those who lived in that place,
New things for God's service to dare.

Then Andrew of Scotland by many revered,
He walked by your side day by day,
Told the story of love of the Saviour most dear,
To all those he met on the way.

So Lord, we would praise you for saints of each age,
Help us, then to follow their lead,
Their stories are written on history's page,
Inspiring each word and each deed.

For St Aidan (31st August)
For Aidan of Lindisfarne,
We give our thanks today,
Remembering his ministry,
To those he met each day.

His generous acts of sharing
The best that he could give,
He gladly gave to others,
And sought for you to live.

To everyone, both rich and poor,
He showed Christ's loving care,
With all those in Northumbria,
The Gospel he would share.

Lord, give to us his patient love
With those we meet each day,
And generous hearts for sharing,
Along the pilgrim way.

Praise

For Music
For the gift of music,
God of harmony, we praise you,
For choirs who lead our worship,
God of harmony, we praise you,
For musicians who turn notes into sound,
God of harmony, we praise you,
For songwriters who put pen to paper,
God of harmony, we praise you,
For orchestras which bring music to life,
God of harmony, we praise you,
For the music of heaven sung by the angels,
God of harmony, we praise you.

You are All
Lord, you are, rest to the weary,
        healing to the sick,
        light to the lost,
        comfort to the sorrowful,
        friend to the lonely,
you are all to all.

O What a Mystery
God of the centuries,
You came to earth for me,
Willing to set me free
From all my sin.
You came to give new life,
To share my joy and strife,
Lord Jesus, Lord of light,
You died for me.
O what a mystery
That you should care for me,
Clothed in humanity,
You came to your world.

Thoughts on Psalm 46
O God, our refuge and our strength,
Our ever present help in time of strife.
Though mountains quake
and oceans roar,
we will not fear, for you are near,
and you will make our city glad –
a place of joy and light.
For you will be there in her midst,
you will bring peace, and make wars cease.
May I be still and know my God.
The day is coming when your name
will be exalted –
even among the heathen.
You, the Lord of hosts, are with us,
now and forevermore.

Thank You, Lord, for Music
Thank you, Lord, for the gift of music – to soothe
            to motivate,
            to inspire,
to transport us to the very gates of heaven,
to bring back memories – both joyous and poignant,
may our lives be a symphony of praise.

Thanksgiving

We Give Thanks
For the sun to warm us,
We give thanks, O Lord,
For the moon to direct us,
We give thanks, O Lord,
For the stars to guide us,
We give thanks, O Lord,
For the rain to refresh us,
We give thanks, O Lord,
For the breeze to cool us,
We give thanks, O Lord,
For your Spirit to fill us,
We give thanks, O Lord.

Count your Blessings
For the beauty of your Creation,
May we count our blessings.
For the freedom which we enjoy,
May we count our blessings.
For an abundance of food to eat,
May we count our blessings.
For warm homes in which to live,
May we count our blessings.
For friends who care about us,
May we count our blessings.
For all your love has given,
May we count our blessings.

May I be Thankful
You have called me by my name,
Lord, I give you thanks.
You have redeemed me,
Lord, I give you thanks.
You bear me up on eagles' wings,
Lord, I give you thanks.
You lead me into pastures green,
Lord, I give you thanks.
You will never leave me,
For this and all your promises,
Lord, I give you thanks.

For All You Give Us
For the gift of each new day,
We thank you, O God.
For nights of sleep,
We thank you, O God.
For the beauty of each sunrise,
We thank you, O God.
For the peace that comes at sunset,
We thank you, O God.
For the seasons of the year,
We thank you, O God.
For the diversity of creation,
We thank you, O God.
For all your gifts to us,
We thank you, O God.

Prayers for Children

Bless Me
Lord of land and sky and sea
Bless a little child like me,
Make me patient, good and strong,
Keep me, Lord, from doing wrong.
Help me live each day for you,
Guide me now in all I do.
Be with me both night and day,
Hear me, Jesus, as I pray.

A Child's Prayer
God of earth and sky and sea,
Bless a little child like me.
Help me follow in your way
As I live from day to day.
Help me, Lord, in all I do
To be honest, kind and true.
Bless me as I go to sleep,
Loving Shepherd of your sheep.
And then, Lord, when I awake,
May I be good for Jesus' sake.
Help me to try to show your love,
And lead me on to heav'n above.

Thank You, God
Thank you, God, for water,
Thank you, God, for rain,
Thank you, God, for sunshine,
To ripen fields of grain.

Thank you, God, for mountains
Reaching to the sky,
Thank you, God, for valleys,
And for deserts dry.

Thank you, God, for oceans
And dolphins swimming free,
Thank you, God, for all the fish
Living in the sea.

Thank you, God, for polar bears
Floating on the ice,
Thank you, God, for elephants
And for tiny mice.

Thank you, God, for what you've made –
All creatures, great and small,
May we protect and care for them,
Because you love them all.

Thanks for Everything
Thank you, God, for little things,
For puppy dogs that play,
And tiny, fluffy kittens,
That seem to sleep all day.

Thank you, God, for woolly lambs,
That skip all through the grass,
And pretty golden daffodils,
I see them as I pass.

Thank you, God, for my warm bed,
I curl up there at night,
With pillow soft, beneath my head,
I sleep till morning light.

Thank you, God, for food to eat
And drink to have as well,
There are so many things you give,
All these your goodness tell.

Thank You for Breakfast
Lord, thank you for the sunshine,
Thank you for the rain,
Thank you for the harvest
And the ripening grain.

Thank you for the cereal
That I eat each day,
Thanks for those who grew it,
Bless them, Lord, I pray.

My Pet has Died
Lord Jesus, my loving dog/cat has died
And I am very sad.
He/she was my dearest friend –
The best I've ever had.
Now, Lord, I feel so lonely
Without him/her here with me,
Please keep him/her safely in your arms,
Take care of him/her for me.

I'm Scared, Lord
Lord Jesus, I am lonely,
Please come and hold my hand.
Lord Jesus, I am hurting,
Just hold me in your arms.
Lord Jesus, I am frightened,
I don't know what to do.
Lord Jesus, come and be with me,
For I feel so alone.
Lord Jesus, you are always near,
Please, hear me when I pray.
Lord Jesus, come and be my Friend
And walk with me each day.

Prayers to be Sung

The Advent Promise
Comfort, comfort, all my people,
Hear the words the prophet told,
Wolf and lamb shall dwell together,
All will rest within one fold.

Every plain shall be exalted,
Every mountain peak brought low,
And in all the desert places,
Cool, refreshing streams will flow.

Cow and bear will eat together,
Goat and leopard be at peace,
And a little child will lead them,
All will share the great King's feast.

Hear the watchword 'Christ is coming'
As a thief within the night,
When he comes, may we be ready
To proclaim him, Lord of light.

Every eye shall then behold him
When he comes to claim his own,
Every knee shall bow before him,
Seated on his sapphire throne.

(Based on the prophecies of Isaiah)
Suggested Tune: Sussex or Halton Holgate

Walk with the Saints

To follow the saints/St ..., Lord, let this be our aim,
To walk in their/his/her footsteps and honour your name,
That seeking to serve those we meet day by day,
May show Christ the Saviour, the Life and the Way.

Then give us their/his/her courage to hold fast the faith,
In quietness and confidence, Lord, may we wait
To see the revealing of your perfect plan,
And in its fulfilment – you own guiding hand.

Grant us their/his/her endurance to run in life's race,
To learn from example that aided by grace,
And standing secure and firm to the end,
In heaven we'll meet you, our Saviour and Friend.

Make us more determined to follow their/his/her lead,
With your grace supplying the strength that we need,
May we, Lord, be willing to die for your word,
'Well done, faithful servant', this message is heard.

Suggested Tune: Slane

Lord of the Saints
Lord, of our Celtic isles we come today,
Praising your name for saints who walked your way,
Give us their faith that we may follow too,
Seeking your will in everything we do.

Lord, of our Celtic isles we ask you now,
As in your presence here we humbly bow,
Fill us with grace and arm us for the fight,
Give us the courage to stand firm for right.

Lord, of our Celtic isles we hold so dear,
Help us to reverence you with holy fear,
That walking in the way your saints have trod,
We may come face to face with you, our God.

Suggested Tune: Highland Cathedral

God the Creator

Lord, you designed each shining constellation,
And flung the stars like diamonds into space,
Yet with such care you made each gene and atom,
God the Creator, of the human race.

You set and placed the planets in their orbits,
Bidding the sun and moon to rise each day,
For only you could fashion all this beauty,
God our Redeemer, be our strength and stay.

You drew the blueprint for each living creature,
And formed them all with tender, loving care,
You made the heavens and earth and nether regions,
God the Designer, of this world so fair.

Suggested Tune: Highwood

A Trust from You
This fragile earth your hands have made,
We hold in trust from you,
Lord, make us ever more aware
Of what we need to do
To cherish its diversity
And treat with loving care,
All plants and birds and wildlife too,
On land or sea or air.

Forgive our greed and our misuse
Of all that you provide
And make us more responsible,
Let conscience be our guide.
For those whose need is very great
Give us concern, we pray,
That peace and justice may abound
In all the world some day.

Help us to value human life
And see your image there.
Lord, grant to us a firm resolve
And readiness to share
That prompted by your guiding hand
In everything we do,
May care and nurture all you made –
It is a trust from you.

Suggested Tune: Kingsfold

The Seasons

For the seasons that you give us
Through the cycle of each year,
We would bring our thanks and worship
As we sing your praises here.
For the early signs of Springtime
As new life is brought to birth,
We would praise your name, O Father,
For the beauty of the earth.

Summer next explodes in colour
In a blaze of every hue,
Trees and plants and every creature,
All unite to worship you.
Once again comes Autumn turning
All the leaves to burnished gold,
May we pause and look in wonder,
At the glory we behold.

Then the icy grip of Winter
Falls upon the dormant land,
Waiting for Spring's resurrection
To begin at your command.
For the seasons that you give us,
Lord, we offer you our praise,
May we hold in trust creation,
Faithful stewards, all our days.

Suggested Tune: Abbotsleigh

Open Our Hearts
Holy Spirit, come inflame us,
With the fire of Pentecost,
Holy Spirit, come endow us,
With the gifts we need the most.

Give us courage and endurance
To pursue the narrow way,
Strengthen patience and obedience,
As we live from day to day.

Fill us with your reassurance,
As we follow where you lead,
May we find your grace sufficient,
To supply our every need.

By our loving and our giving
May we shed your love abroad,
Make us faithful in our living
That your name might be adored.

May our hearts indeed be open,
To your power to change our lives,
May sin's hold on us be broken,
As to heaven our spirits rise.

Suggested Tune: Redhead No 46

Those Who Labour
Jesus Saviour, Lord of pity,
Hear your children when they call,
Look in love on town and city,
Bless your servants, one and all.

Those who labour in the factory
Crafting merchandise to sell,
Be with them in their endeavours,
May they aim to make things well.

Give your wisdom to the doctors
As they seek the sick to heal,
Bless the nurses in their caring
Showing love, sincere and real.

Give compassion and commitment
To all those enforcing law,
May they show your truth and justice
To all people – rich and poor.

Those who work long hours in office
Scanning their computer screens,
May they glimpse the vision glorious
Of your majesty unseen.

Look upon us in our labours
May we seek to bring you praise,
By the manner of our living,
May we serve you all our days.

Suggested Tune: St Andrew

To Find Your Presence
See the rays of light descending
On these walls of ancient stone,
Hear the sound of music blending,
From the earth to heaven's throne.

Here the footsore pilgrim kneeling,
Reaches now their goal at last,
You are gracious in your dealing,
And forgive our sins now past.

And the wandering soul in coming,
Pauses then to stop and pray,
Lord, direct their mindless roaming,
Lead us to eternal day.

Lord, we come for different reasons,
Seeking quiet and peace of mind,
Those who visit through the seasons,
May they here your presence find.

Suggested Tune: Stuttgart

God of Everything

God of all knowledge, I give you my mind,
That waking or sleeping, your peace may I find,
Endow me with wisdom to know what is good,
Then give me the strength, Lord, to live as I should.

God of all loving, I give you my heart,
That caring and sharing, your love may impart,
Fill me with compassion for all those I meet,
And have mercy on me, as I kneel at your feet.

God of all power, I give you my will,
In ready obedience, each task to fulfil,
That moved by your Spirit, in living each day,
May have grace to serve you and to follow your way.

God of all being, I give you my life,
Just help me to trust you in joy and in strife,
That striving and serving you, Lord, to the end,
In heaven you'll greet me – my Saviour and Friend.

Suggested Tune: Slane

Blessings

Day by Day
May the love of Christ enfold you,
May the lives of the saints inspire you,
May the holy angels watch over you,
✠ and the blessing of God …

For a Dear Friend
May God pour down upon you
The riches of his grace,
May he defend you on every side,
May he give you joy in abundance,
May he surround you with his presence,
And may he keep you in his love,
This day and forevermore,
✠ and the blessing of God …

May God Bless You
May the presence of God surround you,
May the love of God enfold you,
And may the wisdom of God guide you,
✠ and may the blessing of God …

May God Guide You
May God the Father who created you,
Guide your footsteps.
May God the Son who redeemed you,
Share your journey.
May God the Holy Spirit who sanctifies you,
Fill every part of your being,
✠ and the blessing of God …

May Christ Bless You
May the Babe of Bethlehem,
Gladden your hearts.
May Christ the Saviour of the world,
Share your earthly pilgrimage.
May Christ the risen Lord,
Welcome you to his Father's house,
✠ and may the blessing of God …

A Birthday Blessing
God bless you on your birthday,
And through each passing year,
May he strengthen, guide and keep you
With his presence ever near.
God grant you health and happiness,
Fulfilment of each dream,
For he is there beside you –
On him your burdens lean.
May he help you and inspire you
As you follow in his way,
For he will surely bless you,
As you live for him each day.

We Ask Your Blessing
May the sunshine of your love, warm us,
May the rain from heaven, cleanse us,
May the rushing, mighty wind, fill us,
✠ and the blessing of God, Creator, Redeemer
and Sanctifier be with us now and always.

A Christmas Blessing
May the joy of the Christ Child
make our hearts glad.
May the glory of the risen Lord
guide our footsteps.
And may Christ, our ascended King,
Lead us to the heavenly places,
✠ and the blessing of God …

At Easter
May Christ risen from the dead
give you new hope
and the assurance of eternal life.
May the risen Lord, light your path
with his resurrection glory
and lead you on the pilgrim way,
✠ and the blessing of God …

An Easter Blessing
May the crucified Saviour draw you to himself,
May the risen Christ fill you with resurrection joy,
May the ascended King, give you life eternal,
✠ and may the blessing of God. …